Babylon
in Europe

Babylon in Europe

What Bible prophecy reveals about the European Union

David Hathaway

New Wine Press

New Wine Ministries
PO Box 17
Chichester
West Sussex
United Kingdom
PO19 2AW

ISBN 1-903725-82-8

Typeset by CRB Associates, Potterhanworth, Lincolnshire
Printed in Malta

Contents

Introduction: Is This Prophetic?

I make no claim to be a prophet, nor to prophesy over individuals. However, I do believe that God has, through the ministry of the Holy Spirit, given me a revelation which I believe to be not only scriptural but vitally important for today. For example – the fall of the Iron Curtain, which the Lord revealed to me some years in advance in 1986 – and which I acted on, in fact founded my present ministry on – in faith! Or more recently the revelations over what the Bible has to say about the EU – and Islam.

For twenty years I have been seeking, with the anointing of the Holy Spirit, to relate what the Bible says in prophecy to current world events. The Word of God is not just old history, nor future predictions to be fulfilled over hundreds of years, but relates directly to the very present time in which we live. If you believe, as I do, that we are literally in the 'last days' – then we are living in the fulfilment of those age-old prophecies. This means that the 'seer', or modern prophet, 'sees' and understands that world events are unfolding *as it was spoken by the prophets . . . '* Just as in the days of Jesus the Scripture said, *'in order to fulfil the words of the prophet, Jesus did . . . '*

However, I have always said that I believe Scripture will be fulfilled in an unusual way – so often unexpected – not as many people thought. Certainly in my life this is so. I do not believe that we shall fully understand Bible prophecy until after the event – sadly for many, not until after Christ has come back!

We are no different from the first disciples – they were eagerly expecting the return of Christ and His Kingdom on earth, but Jesus rebuked them, reminded them that first they must receive the Holy Spirit, that after the Holy Spirit came on them they would then receive power and become witnesses to the Gospel – and this should be our primary focus too. Jesus had spoken about the promised Holy Spirit many times during His ministry, but only when the Holy Spirit actually fell on the day of Pentecost did the disciples fully understand the Scripture. As Peter said, *'This is what was spoken by the prophet Joel'* (Acts 2:16). So he began to evangelise and won 3,000 for Christ that first day!

Because we are like the disciples, this is why, when writing, I often ask questions and challenge you to find the answers. But I also believe that if we, as Christians, want to impact our nations, we must have an understanding of the times we are living in.

When we see what is happening in the world today, the fulfilment of so many Bible prophecies, most significantly the rebirth of Israel as a nation in May 1948, and how close we are to the return of Christ, we need to act fast. Remember the Great Commission of Christ: *'Go into all the world and preach the gospel to every creature'* (Mark 16:15). Remember also that the Bible says: *'For this purpose the Son of God was manifested, that He might destroy the works of the devil'* (1 John 3:8). In order for us to participate in these things and to see the fulfilment of all that God, rather than the devil, wants to do in these last days, we need God's vision. As the Bible says: *'Where there is no vision, the people perish'* (Proverbs 29:18 KJV) – they don't know where to go, what to do.

This is why I write about the European Union – and the beast which will soon toss her aside; world powers and world government; terrorism ... I show you these things to challenge you to question what is happening, to pray – and to **act**!

If I am correct in my understanding of world events, then we are challenged to evangelise and win the world with great urgency. If I am wrong, we have more time, but at least the sense of urgency will stir us up to seek the outpouring of God's Spirit and we will evangelise now – and we will achieve more. If I am right, then those who are asleep, wrapped up in the cares of this world, or merely interested in prophecy for its own sake, will be left behind. The parable of the five wise and five foolish virgins is a terrible warning.

Jesus is coming very quickly, sooner than most realise.

Why the European Union?

The whole question of the European Union is creating much interest and debate in Britain and worldwide, which leads me to ask why this pressure has come in the twenty-first century to create a European Union, a European Empire, which has never previously existed. Of course, that does not mean it should not exist, but I ask what the reason behind it is. Is there some hidden purpose in creating it?

One argument is that it is to prevent war in Europe, which has never been united but has a history of division into tribes and nations, all of which have changed borders, usually because of conquest. Even the Romans failed to unite more than part, prevented by the Huns, the Slavs and were ultimately defeated by the Germanic tribes. Not even the might of Charlemagne or Napoleon or latterly Hitler could achieve this Union, although all tried.

What is behind the creation of a single European State? You can look at it from a political, social or an economic point of view, but don't dismiss the possibility that there could actually be a biblical background to this. Could the European Union be the fulfilment of something which was foreseen more than 3,000 years ago in the prophecies of the Bible, in the book of Daniel?

Dream and interpretation given to Nebuchadnezzar, King of Babylon

'You, O king, were watching; and behold, a great image! This great image, whose splendor was excellent, stood before you; and its form was awesome. This image's head was of fine gold, its chest and arms of silver, its belly and thighs of bronze, its legs of iron, its feet partly of iron and partly of clay. You watched while a stone was cut out without hands, which struck the image on its feet of iron and clay, and broke them in pieces. Then the iron, the clay, the bronze, the silver, and the gold were crushed together, and became like chaff from the summer threshing floors; the wind carried them away so *that no trace of them was found. And the stone that struck the image became a great mountain and filled the whole earth.*

This is the dream. Now we will tell the interpretation of it before the king.

You, O king [Nebuchadnezzar, of Babylon], *are a king of kings. For the God of heaven has given you a kingdom, power, strength, and glory . . . you are this head of gold. But after you shall arise another kingdom inferior to yours; then another, a third kingdom of bronze, which shall rule over all the earth. And the fourth kingdom shall be as strong as iron, inasmuch as iron breaks in pieces and shatters everything; and like iron that crushes, that kingdom will break in pieces and crush all the others. Whereas you saw the feet and toes, partly of potter's clay and partly of iron, the kingdom shall be divided; yet the strength of the iron shall be in it, just as you saw the iron mixed with ceramic clay. And as the toes of the feet were partly of iron and partly of clay, so the kingdom shall be partly strong and partly fragile. As you saw iron mixed with ceramic clay . . . they will not adhere to one another, just as iron does not mix with clay.*

And in the days of these kings the God of heaven will set up a kingdom which shall never be destroyed; and the kingdom shall not be left to other people; it shall break in pieces and consume all these kingdoms, and it shall stand forever. Inasmuch as you saw that the stone was cut out of the mountain without hands, and that it broke in pieces the iron, the bronze, the clay, the silver, and the gold – the great God has made known to the king what will come to pass after this. The dream is certain, and its interpretation is sure.'

(Daniel 2:31–45; circa 605–530 BC)

The Road to European Union

The dream of a united Europe is as old as Europe itself – from the times of the Roman Empire, then under Charlemagne, the Holy Roman Empire with its Prince-Bishops, Napoleon and finally Hitler. Every attempt failed because they relied on military oppression. Finally, following Hitler's World War, 1939–45, Europe lay shattered.

Divided Europe

The infamous 1945 Yalta Conference was called to settle the future of the ruined continent. Joseph Stalin – the Soviet Leader – took control of East Germany and all the East European states, leaving West Germany to the Americans, French and British. This was the first political shot fired in what would become known as the Cold War. Two alliances underpinned the hostilities: the North Atlantic Treaty Organisation (NATO), formed by the West European and North American countries in 1949, and the Warsaw Pact, created by the Union of Soviet Socialist Republics and the East European countries in 1955. It was Winston Churchill who described this divide as the descent of an 'Iron Curtain'.

From 1945 defeated Germany was divided into Soviet, US, British and French occupation zones. Berlin, deep in the Soviet zone, was divided in the same way. In June 1948 Soviet forces blocked entry to the city from the West, and then in 1961, the communist East German regime erected the Berlin Wall, isolating the East and Western sectors of the city.

The East

For four full decades the Soviet Communist Party kept East Germany and all Eastern Europe under its iron grip – brutally suppressing uprisings in various places, until 1985 when Mikhail Gorbachev came to power in Russia. Facing economic problems at home, as well as nationalist unrest in all East Europe, he introduced a course of reform which he called *glasnost* (openness) and *perestroika* (restructuring). In 1989, the year that the Iron Curtain dividing Europe began to collapse, the first Soviet parliament since 1918 was held.

The fall of the Berlin Wall marked the Cold War's psychological end – the formal announcement was made in the Conference on Security and Co-operation in 1990. During the conference, attended by the European Countries, USSR, Canada and USA, a declaration was made that the era of confrontation and the division of Europe had ended, and that their relations would now be founded on respect and cooperation.

In 1991, following the demise of the USSR and an attempted coup against Gorbachev, Boris Yeltsin was elected Russian president and a new body, the Commonwealth of Independent States, was formed. The communist system was uprooted by private enterprise and a mafia 'market' economy. Prices soared and savings were wiped out overnight. Since then, Russia has struggled to build a democratic political system and free market. While some progress has been made on the economic front, recent years have seen a growing recentralisation of power under Russian President Vladimir Putin.

The West

The sudden demise of strict, uniform Soviet control over the individual states of Eastern Europe resulted in a mirror-opposite in

Western Europe – just as suddenly, the European Community was irreversibly propelled towards an ever-increasing economic and political union. At the same time, the former satellite communist countries turned to the European Community for political and economic assistance – the EC agreed to supply aid to many of these countries, but would not to allow them to join immediately.

In response to this rapid political upheaval in the East, Germany (now reunited for the first time since the war) and France proposed an intergovernmental conference to pursue closer European integration. The 1991 Treaty on European Union – commonly known as the Maastricht Treaty – was signed, founding the modern EU.

Formally established on 1st November 1993 the European Union is the most recent in a series of European organisations that originated in 1951 with the European Coal and Steel Community, an association of six European nations whose aim was to rebuild the blighted economies of post-war Europe by pooling resources. Six years later, in 1957, they signed the Treaty of Rome to become the European Economic Community (EEC). This in turn evolved into the European Community (EC) in 1967.

The objective of European unity has been, from the beginning, to promote and expand cooperation among member states in economic, trade and social issues, in security, defence and international foreign policy, and in judicial matters. Under the Maastricht Treaty, European Citizenship was granted to the citizens of all member states. Border controls were relaxed, and customs and immigration agreements were modified to allow European citizens greater freedom to live, work, and study in any of the member states.

Economic union – the real goal

Economic integration has been a major goal of the EU from its inception as the European Coal and Steel Community – it was never a question of 'if', but 'when'. The principle of economic and monetary union was well advanced by the late 1960s, and in 1979 the Economic Monetary System (EMS) was established. The next major step was the implementation of the Economic and Monetary Union (EMU) in the 1990s, followed by the single European currency, the euro. In January 2002, the euro replaced the national currencies of twelve member states. As of 2006 thirteen EU countries still do not participate in the single currency: they are Denmark, Sweden, Great Britain and the ten states that joined the EU in 2004 (these ten states are committed to joining the euro, but none will do so before 2007). From the introduction of the EMU, EU members were driven to an unprecedented level of integration and cooperation. Yet there was a growing concern among European citizens and some EU member governments that the major EU institutions – especially the all-powerful, unelected European Commission – were neither democratic nor accountable. As the powers of the EU grew, so did worries that the Commission had become a bureaucracy exercising too much control with too little oversight at the expense of the only democratically elected institution of the EU, the European Parliament – a mere 'rubber stamp' to the decisions of the unelected Commission.

Post-war dreams for a European Union were politically and economically motivated – the political motive was the conviction that only a consenting, intergovernmental organisation could finally bring to an end the succession of wars which have so troubled Europe since the collapse of the Roman Empire. Some supporters of European political unity further believed that if the nations of Europe were to assume a dominant role in world affairs, they had to speak with one voice and command resources comparable to those of the United States. The economic motive ostensibly rested on the belief that larger markets would lead to greater productivity and higher standards of living. Economic and political viewpoints merged in the fact that economic strength is the basis of political and military power. As most European countries were hesitant to surrender control over national affairs, most of the practical proposals for intergovernmental organisations understood that economic integration must precede political unification.

United Kingdom and Europe

In the preliminaries to the 1957 Treaty of Rome, the United Kingdom was invited to join the European Economic Community. However, the UK refused because it objected to the loss of control over national policies implied in European integration, and instead attempted to persuade European neighbours to create a simple free-trade area. After the EEC was ratified, the UK along with six other European nations created the European Free Trade Association (EFTA). The EFTA treaty provided only for the elimination of tariffs on industrial products between member nations – unlike the EEC, EFTA members could withdraw at any time. But in view of the EEC's apparent economic success, in 1961 the United Kingdom began negotiations toward EEC membership; however, membership was vetoed twice by France because of Britain's close relationship to the United States. The UK finally joined the EEC on 1st January 1973, despite much popular opposition.

Is This the End of the EU?

With so much debate regarding the European Union, I need to remind readers that it is more than eight years (1998) since God began to reveal to me the truth of what the Bible says about the European Union. Now we have unfolding in front of us the confirmation of Daniel's vision and my prophetic warning of the true nature of the EU.

The three major and significant links between the EU and Bible prophecy are:

1. The European Parliament building in Strasbourg is deliberately designed in the shape of the Tower of Babel in Genesis, a symbol of rebellion against God, who destroyed it and confused the languages. The EU say that they want to restore and finish what God destroyed.

2. The image in Nebuchadnezzar's vision (Daniel 2) which Daniel translated, clearly showed five world empires, all of which, except the last – the feet of iron mixed with clay – were fulfilled during the biblical period ending with the Roman Empire in the time of Christ. The last part of the image, the feet of iron and clay, is the restored Roman Empire – the Treaty of Rome. This Roman Empire, fractured, unable to form real unity, is the EU, exactly as we have it today – the Bible shows it as iron and clay which do not mix. In the words first used by President George Bush Snr, 'Old Europe and

New Europe'. Or, as President Chirac of France said, 'Anglo-Saxon v. Federal Eurocrats'.

3. The continent of Europe took its actual name from the woman in Greek mythology who was raped by the god Jupiter, who took the form of a bull, then afterwards the woman herself became the 'Queen of Heaven'. The EU uses the symbol of this woman on the beast (also described in Revelation 17) everywhere: from Brussels to the Berlin Wall – from the old Deutschmark to the new euro coin – from postage stamps to an old German telephone card.

During the campaigning for the French referendum on the Constitution in 2005, the 'yes' campaigners said a 'no' vote would be a rejection, not just of the Constitution, but the entire European project. Did they speak the truth? If so, then the EU is dead. Or did they distort the truth? Then this is an admission that the whole theology of the EU is based on untruth and an inability to accept what the voters said.

The Constitution was actually signed by the heads of the twenty-five nations of the EU in October 2004 in Rome, where the EU was first launched in 1957. This was done, not so much to make the EU work better, as to lock in the vision of federalisation before the ten newly elected member states made it more difficult to do so. The decisive 'no' votes in Holland and particularly France exposed the dislike of the 'Anglo-Saxon' direction of Europe and the inability of the 'Old European Federalists' to survive competition from the low-cost economies of the 'New European Anglo-Saxons'. But this in turn ignores the far greater threat from the emerging Asian economies, first in India, and now even more so in the world's largest and fastest growing economy, China.

One interesting outcome of the French 'no' to the Constitution is that the Prime Minister was quickly replaced by Dominique de Villepin, who is the first wholehearted admirer of Napoleon to become head of a French government since Napoleon III in 1848! This should be a warning, not only to the British who defeated the first Napoleon in 1814, but also to Russia, where he was the first 'European visionary' to be militarily ejected from Russia in 1812, followed almost in identical fashion by another 'European visionary', Adolf Hitler, 130 years later. Let that be a warning to those who see the dream of a united Europe extending from the Atlantic to the Ural Mountains – as some do! President Putin in Moscow re-named the Kievsky Square where the main Moscow-Kiev railway station is situated as the 'Europa Square', complete with the 'woman on the beast' (donated by Brussels) and representation of the national flags of Europe as the tower of Babel.

Surprisingly even in the centre of Europe the reality of the problems of a single currency, the euro, has appeared. At the end of May 2005, an Italian government minister was the first, followed by three other top figures, who calculated that Italy was in such a deep crisis that they saw the advantage of a revolt against the euro. At the same time, when the German bankers and the Italians talk of coming out of the euro (and the German magazine *Stern* advised readers to check their euro notes, commenting that the notes issued in Germany begin with X and those issued in Italy with S), it is beginning to cross German and other northern European minds that they might be better off outside the euro currency.

The effect of the introduction of the 'euro-dollar' has been to weaken the economy of Germany until it is worse than at any time since the last war, with unemployment over 10% and more than five million out of work. In France the threat of the incoming ten former Soviet states is that manufacturing will move to Poland or Slovenia where labour costs are a sixth, and has even brought Italy to the point of insolvency. The threat given to us in the UK was that if we did not join the single currency we would become like Norway or Switzerland. Both these have prospered outside the euro zone – and surprise – we in UK have also prospered more than those who accepted blindly, without the option of a vote. In 2002 Sir Alan Walters, who was adviser to Margaret Thatcher, predicted that the euro would collapse within five years. Now we can add to that the failure of the stability pact, and the 'no' vote from France and Holland to the EU Constitution, which removes the stability from the currency. It might become worthless without a Constitution to back it.

So what of the future? Daniel's vision says that this unequal, crumbling union will last until Christ returns. It is no use praying that the EU will break up – the Bible says this will only happen at the return of Christ – rather pray for His quick return:

> '... *as you saw the iron mixed with baked clay, so the people will be a mixture and will not remain united ...*'
>
> (Daniel 2:43 NIV)

> '*In the time of those kings, the God of heaven will set up a kingdom ... It will crush all those kingdoms and bring them to an end ...*'
>
> (Daniel 2:44 NIV)

French President, Chirac, said that the EU Constitution would complete the French Revolution. Thank God, history reminds us that only the Wesleyan Revival saved Britain from this bloodbath crossing the Channel and coming to our shores. The British are the second largest contributors to the EU budget, but 46% of the EU income goes on the Common Agricultural Policy (CAP), which prevents the world trading with us and supplying cheap food – it acts against the African countries, who could gain more from trading with us, as India and now China do, than by all the talk of debt reduction and food aid. You do not rescue poorer nations by making them totally dependent on aid; you need them to create wealth within their own economy. If you feed a hungry man today, tomorrow he will still be hungry. If you enable him to grow crops, catch fish or own livestock – he will feed himself and his family.

We need to realise that the EU is part of the preparation for the rise of the False Prophet and the Antichrist. The basis of the EU is a totally secular federal system, where evangelicals are called sects, to be marginalised and neutralised so that they cannot preach biblical truth or declare that the only way of salvation is through

Christ for fear of 'racialism' and offending other faiths. The danger of this assumption is that Islam becomes regarded as a mainstream faith equal to Catholicism – and the evangelicals are the sects. Note that Islam is never called a sect! Bible-based faith is!

Totalitarianism flourishes on poverty, as happened in Germany in the 1930s with the rise of Hitler, after the collapse of the Weimar Republic, and as is happening now in Russia, where the pensioners and unemployed march in the streets demanding the return of communism and the rehabilitation of Stalin! Economic collapse in the EU will open the door for the rise of the 'False Prophet', and the 'Antichrist' as leader.

Today we desperately need real leadership in the UK if we want God to heal our land. It would be wonderful if we could have a political leader with spiritual insight – but where are our Christian leaders who will lead us back to God as a nation – a Christian with enough leadership and charisma who can influence a significant minority?

Two hundred years ago in Britain, God dealt with a state church which had become political and institutionalised, by the birth of Methodism and a spiritual revival. God dealt with drunkenness and crime in Britain, worse than we have today, through the preaching of the Gospel and the message of the Salvation Army. One hundred and fifty years ago this happened in Russia to the Russian Orthodox Church, which had become a puppet of the state, with a non-conformist revival under Lord Radstock from Britain.

Only a spiritual revival can save Britain today. Mainstream churches seem powerless and silent in the face of a society which slips daily further into sin and rebellion against God. Pray that God will raise up strong and fearless leaders who will call for a return to the authority of God's Word, and put a stop to the cult of putting man's tradition before God's authority!

Child of the French Revolution?

In 2005 the people of France voted 'no' to the European Constitution; they were afraid that the socialism they, as a nation, believe in was not at the heart of this document. In his desperate battle for a yes vote, President Chirac made this strong appeal: 'The European Constitution is the pure child of the French Revolution!'

Child of the French Revolution? What did he mean?

For ten years, from 1789 to 1799, a bloody political upheaval took place in France that was to change the face of Europe – right up until this present day. It was *no* to the monarchy, *no* to the church and *no* to the existing fabric of society. In the midst of terror, mob rule and execution by guillotine, in the name of 'liberty, equality, fraternity', it was *yes* to a totally new socialist constitution and charter of human rights. *Yes* to man, *no* to God.

All this was in response to a crisis of injustice, oppression, and high taxes. Led by thinkers of the 'Enlightenment', the Assembly of Commoners did the unthinkable, overturned the established order of the nation and declared themselves equal to the ruling nobility and clergy. On 14th July 1789 the loathed royal fortress of the Bastille in Paris was stormed. 'This is a riot,' said the King. 'No, Sire, this is a revolution!'

France with its revolutionary socialist ideology seemed set to sweep away the old order in all Europe, until by 1792, Austria, Prussia, Britain, Holland and Spain were at war with France. But the anti-God French Revolution never did overwhelm Britain as feared. Why? Because of the preaching of the Wesley brothers and because of the revival of a healthy, practical, life-changing faith which they brought to the whole nation. Even our secular history books acknowledge this.

The Revolution was based on a radical concept – socialism. A new world order born out of the intellectual philosophy of the 'Enlightenment'. It rejected God and everything to do with religion and the old structure of society, replacing faith in God with the 'light' of human reason. Man in control – atheism. President Chirac proudly described France as the riverbed, the source of atheism – and this is what we have at the heart of the European Union, a core rejection of God which began in France!

The first group of so-called 'Illuminati' – 'Enlightened Ones' – convened in 1776 to formulate this revolutionary socialism and rejection of God which was to overturn France in 1789. But did you know that out of this socialism, communism was developed? It was the same movement of 'Illuminati' which formed the Communist League in 1847, commissioned Marx to write the Communist Manifesto in 1848, and then launched the campaign for International Communism from New York in 1859. Did you know that the 1917 Russian Revolution was financed from Europe and America? Did you know that the seventy years Russia spent without God under communism was foreign to, and an imposition on, the Russian soul? This is why, with the fall of communism in 1989, exactly two hundred years after the French Revolution, there is the beginning of such a great revival of faith there now. No other country in Europe has such a hunger for God as Russia.

No to God – *Yes* to humanism and reason!

If the European Constitution is the 'pure child of the French Revolution' as Chirac said, this is why there is no mention of our Judeo-Christian God and why it is so seriously flawed.

Indeed French humanist, former President Valery Giscard d'Estaing, had these words included in the Constitution:

> '...Europe is a continent that has brought forth civilisation ... its inhabitants, arriving in successive waves since the beginning of time, have gradually developed over the centuries the values that are the foundation of humanism: equality of all humans, liberty, respect for reason...'

The Constitution, in its introduction, names Greek and Roman civilisations as the formative traditions of Europe. Does this then identify Europe as the successor to the Babylonian/Greek/Roman empires of Daniel 2 – in rebellion against God and against the people of God – with the feet of the statue that will be smashed by Christ's return?

The EU may be godless, it may be in rebellion, but it likes to say that it is a community of 'values'. Some of its values have in fact sprung from its former Christian faith, but many can be traced back to the humanistic Greek civilisation which was so decadent at the time of Christ. A code of 'Human Rights' (modelled on the 'Declaration of the Rights of Man' produced by the French Revolution in 1789) now replaces the simple Ten Commandments of the Word of God.

Romans 1:21–32 warns that when men fail to honour God – though they believe themselves to be wise and reasonable – their hearts become darkened and they become fools; when men call God a lie, and honour created man rather than the Creator, they open themselves to every vile and perverse thing. God's values are lost.

German intercessor for Europe, Ortwin Schweitzer, wrote on the internet:

> 'The optimism of the eighteenth-century "Enlightenment" can be pardoned for its belief in reason. But it is unforgivable to offer this optimistic faith [in reason] to a Europe that has gone through two World Wars and the Holocaust, despite placing reason on the throne in every area. This is why, after

the horror of the Third Reich, the fathers of the German Constitution included God in their Constitution. They felt only people who were guided by pleasing the God of the Bible and living accordingly, could ensure peace and liberty in Europe.'

The fact that there are several religions in Europe – and likely to be more in the future – is an argument cited for leaving the word 'Christian' out of the Constitution. This decision was opposed by new EU-member Poland, but welcomed by EU-hopeful Turkey, who together with Europe's existing fourteen million Moslems, resents the EU's image as a 'Christian Club'.

Historically, from the Crusades, to the Inquisition, to the Holocaust, European Christianity is guilty of sin – but the origin of these crimes cannot be found in the teachings of Jesus Christ, only in man himself. Islam, as found in Muhammad's teachings, is aggressive: following Muhammad's own example in the Koran, its goal is to build a worldwide god-state for Allah, the 'House of Islam', to gain the predominance of power everywhere, by any means, including deceit (peace agreements that are made only to be broken at a more advantageous time, Surah 9:1) and *jihad* (terror and war, Surah 9:3, 5, 11). This is why Chirac is afraid that the 'riverbed of European atheism' may yet be 'flooded by Islam'.

Whilst there is a fear of Islam in Europe, there is also a strong desire not to offend. Yet Europe is becoming more and more actively intolerant of Christianity: in Britain, some local education authorities are refusing to allow Christmas plays and concerts. One attempted to ban 'Hot Cross Buns' in school (just a tasty traditional food with a white pastry cross made in Lent); and Leicester hospital authority contemplated removing bedside Bibles from the hospitals. There are more and more laws restricting the preaching of the Gospel, especially on TV. You cannot say that Jesus is the only way to God. The European Union even rejected Roman Catholic Buttiglione as Europe Justice Commissioner because he privately expressed his Bible-based views on homosexuality and unmarried mothers.

Where is Babel Today?

'... by your sorcery all the nations were deceived!'

(Revelation 18:23)

An official poster, released by the Council of Europe to promote European Unity, depicted a modern-day Tower of Babel being built by the peoples of Europe, with the slogan, 'Many Tongues, One Voice'. What kind of statement is Europe making about itself?

In the beginning God created man, blessed him, commanded him to rule the earth and gave him dominion over every living thing (Genesis 1:27–28) – even over the serpent! But the serpent, making evil appear to be good, incited Adam and Eve to rebel against God saying, 'You will be like God' (Genesis 3:5). This first seed of wickedness multiplied as one generation succeeded another until there was so much violence and corruption that God grieved that He had ever made man. There was no alternative but to destroy the earth by a flood and begin again through Noah and his family (Genesis 6:5–22).

After the flood Noah's descendants increased – but among them was Nimrod (meaning 'Rebel'). Described as a hunter – maybe not just of animals, but figuratively also of men – he became very powerful, just like the wicked generation before the flood. He made Babylon (Babel) the centre of his kingdom and of his rebellion against God (Genesis 10:8–10). Here, in order to increase in power (literally, to 'make themselves a name') the people joined together to build a great city, with a temple-tower reaching the skies.

It was as if the city and the tower represented a political and spiritual system of control even in those days, a union of men and spiritual forces that was opposed to God. God saw their intentions and what they had begun to do 'as one' (politically united) and with one language. If it continued, there would be no restraining them from doing whatever they wanted (Genesis 11:6). God **had** to destroy the city and its tower.

> 'So the LORD scattered them . . . and they ceased building the city. Therefore its name is called Babel [confusion], because there the LORD confused the language of all the earth.'
>
> (Genesis 11:8–9)

If we have another world government which will re-create Babel and seek to reverse the division of languages until they speak as one, does this infer that God must again intervene and prevent man's rebellion by destroying this Babel?

The next thing we see, in Genesis 12, is God beginning **His** Kingdom on earth through Abraham. But the story of Babel (also known as 'Babylon'), is not finished even today. We see God's irrevocable hatred and judgement of Babylon (Babel) as a haunt of demons throughout the Bible. In 586 BC God allowed His **own** people, the children of Abraham, to be hunted down and driven into exile in Babylon because of their constant rebellion against Him!

Here in exile God showed His servant Daniel the mystery of Babylon, a world power beginning under the headship of Babylon, but continuing down through the generations under other names, in other places, until at last God brings them all to an end and establishes His Kingdom for ever (Daniel 2:31–45). In the light of history, the generally accepted interpretation of Daniel's vision of the statue is that the Babylonian Empire (gold head) was followed by the Medo-Persian Empire (silver), the Greek (bronze) and then the Roman Empire (iron) which would lead to the final world power as a possible re-constituted Roman Empire (the ten toes being a mixture of iron and clay). The original six nations that signed the Treaty of Rome in 1957 now total twenty-five – but there is another organisation called the Club of Rome, formed in 1968, with the blueprint to establish world government by dividing the world into ten regions – and this is being fulfilled right now.

The Roman Empire was the greatest of the ancient world, lasting for more than six centuries. Finally in AD 395 it divided into East and West, beginning the fulfilment of Daniel's prophecy that it would not remain united – as with the two legs of the image (Daniel 2:41–43). The Eastern Roman Empire made its capital in Constantinople (modern Istanbul), becoming the seat of the Orthodox Church, and it continued until overthrown by the Moslem Turks in 1453. In the West, the last of the Roman Emperors abdicated in AD 476, but significantly the power passed from the secular empire of Rome into the Catholic Church and the Popes of Rome nevertheless went on to crown many 'Holy Roman Emperors'. The dream of re-uniting all Europe has endured down through the centuries; it was the same vision which in the past inspired Napoleon, Hitler – and today the European Union.

But who is the prophetic successor to the Roman Empire that Daniel described? Where is its spiritual and political power located? Could it be that the United States, which was settled by Europeans, inherited the Babylonian mantle? Or has it passed to the United Nations? Could its seat be in a United Europe which includes the former communist countries? Could it be Moslem Turkey as it seeks to join the EU, or possibly Russia? Or is it yet to be revealed?

This vision of a Europe united as the centre of world power has at times come close to reality. The Romans, at the peak of their world power, controlled Europe from the Mediterranean to the North of England, from the Pyrenees to the Black Forest. Unable to conquer the tribes of Germany, these formed the eastern horde that eventually sacked Rome and ended its empire.

From then on the dream for control of Europe and world power was fought over by the French and German peoples. Charlemagne (AD 742–841), king of the Franks, seized the northern part of Italy, Rome, and the Germanic kingdoms of Saxony and Bavaria, and was crowned Holy Roman Emperor by the Pope in AD 800; after his death his empire fragmented. The title of Holy Roman Emperor then fell to the Germanic princes and the Hapsburg dynasty that controlled much of Europe (Germany, Austria, Italy, Spain, Luxembourg, and the Netherlands) until Napoleon seized the dream, forcing the Pope to crown him Emperor in France in 1804, whilst he ravaged most of Europe, reaching as far as Moscow. Germany's Bismarck and Kaiser Wilhelm II were the next with World War I, followed by Hitler and World War II and his dream of the Third Reich (kingdom).

In 1948 the 'Council of Europe' – a new institution created to finally fulfil the dream of a united Europe – met for the first time in Strasbourg. The city straddles formerly disputed German/French territory – the Germans and French having fought against each other for the control of Europe for hundreds of years, ever since the fall of the Roman Empire in the fifth century AD.

Opened in 2000 as a symbol of European political unity, the striking new European Parliament Building in Strasbourg is modelled on Brueghel's famous 'Tower of Babel' painting. Brueghel, who used his paintings to depict religious themes, modelled the tower on the shape of the ruins of the Colosseum in Rome, in order to emphasise not only God's judgement on the Babylonian Empire, but also on the Roman Empire! This begs the question – is the EU the spiritual descendant of the original Babel, and is the EU attempting to rebuild what God once destroyed? The Tower of Babel/Babylon in the Bible was a system of world government that seemed good to men, but was in fact raised in opposition to God. When God saw men united against Him, He confused their speech so that they could no longer conspire together in one language, and they were forced to stop building their diabolical political system (Genesis 11).

When looked at from the *outside*, the new building in Strasbourg represents the Tower of Babel, and from the *inside* the Colosseum – Babylon *and* Rome! This connection did not escape the careful attention of the architects – when entered, the building has an oval area open to the sky, precisely like the Colosseum! It is important to know that the Colosseum in Rome was built to celebrate the destruction of the Jewish Temple in Jerusalem in AD 70, and was opened in AD 80 with games lasting one hundred days. Most of the ten thousand men who took part were killed and five thousand animals were massacred. Many early Christians were later martyred there and thrown to the wild beasts.

An American who heard me speaking about the strange new parliament building was impressed by the Holy Spirit that there is a lot more to Strasbourg than initially realised: he found out that on 14th February 1349 Strasbourg was the scene of the first mass massacre by fire of Jews in Europe. Collectively accused of causing the Black Death by poisoning the local water supplies, two thousand men, women and children were herded into a circle and burned alive. A few who accepted forcible baptism were spared, but many of these were then massacred a few months later when the Black Death reached the gates of Strasbourg itself. On 12th September 1349 Holy Roman Emperor Charles IV issued a decree clearing the town of any guilt for this massacre of the Jews and the plunder of their possessions – but two calls upon the horn, played nightly until the French Revolution, perpetuated the memory of the supposed treason of those innocent Jews.

It is a very interesting architectural feature that from the epicentre of the open inner courtyard of the new Parliament Building radiates a dark line growing wider until it reaches a large gap created in the otherwise complete outer wall with a view directly to Strasbourg Cathedral in the distance. The Archbishop of Strasbourg at the time of the massacre was an arch-anti-semitic.

This massacre by fire in Strasbourg set a vile precedent for European anti-semitism – preminiscent of the Nazi Holocaust where six million Jews died in Hitler's gas ovens. How significant in prophecy if the Tower of Babel in Strasbourg is built on the ashes of these Jews. Remember God's irrevocable promise to Abraham and all his Jewish descendants in Genesis 12:3:

> *'I will bless those who bless you,*
> *And I will curse him who curses you.'*

Another symbol adopted by Europe, as curious as the Tower of Babel, is the Greek myth of the 'Rape of Europa' (the Greek word *Europa* is translated in English as 'Europe'). In every case a wanton woman, Europa, can be seen riding a beast (Revelation 17:1–7; note especially that the forehead of the woman riding the beast here in the Bible is branded with the name, 'Mystery Babylon'). The mythical story is that Zeus, the father of the gods, spied Europa alone on the beach and lusted after her. He transformed himself into a bull of dazzling whiteness with horns like a crescent moon and lay down at her feet. She climbed on his back and he plunged with her into the waves of the sea before raping her. Europa conceived a son, and after her death she received divine honour as 'Queen of Heaven', whilst the bull, as a god, returning into heaven, dissolved into the constellation in the sky known as Taurus.

The Brussels and Strasbourg EU Parliaments both contain statues and paintings of this woman on the beast. Outside the Council of Europe building in Brussels is a crude sculpture of this evil scarlet woman, riding the beast. This same symbol is found in many other statues and paintings, one found in the airport lounge in Brussels; on stamps; a German phone card; on an old five Deutschmark banknote and even today on the euro currency. The symbol even appeared on a painting near the Berlin Wall.

Another (subtle) indication of this symbolism is the European flag – blue with twelve stars in a circle. The man who designed it was inspired by the twelve stars that in Roman Catholic tradition halo the head of Mary. He still hopes Mary will one day be incorporated into the design – the Pope has consecrated the whole of Europe (including Russia) to her. So the actual flag is of the 'Queen of Heaven' (as the Catholics call Mary), now as the 'Queen of Europe', at the very centre of the EU – but the title 'Queen of Heaven' was given to Europa, the mythical woman who was raped by the bull (Zeus) whose pagan star sign is Taurus!

This makes me ask – is Europe today being raped politically/ financially/spiritually – if so, by whom?

The Gateway to Hell

Six hundred years before Christ, after years of rebellion against God, the Jewish people were driven captive from Jerusalem – the city God had chosen – into exile in Babylon, the haunt of demons, sorceries and spells, the very place chosen by the devil, Lucifer, first to deceive Adam and Eve into rebellion against God in the Garden of Eden, then to establish his world government in order to lift up his head against God (Genesis 2 & 3; 11:1–7; Isaiah 14:4–24; 47; Jeremiah 51:9; Revelation 18).

Psalm 137 tells us that the exiles wept by the rivers of Babylon when they remembered Zion (Jerusalem). Why? Because in Hebrew numerology, the hidden meaning of Babel (Babylon) is 'separation' – from God! In Babylon was the 'ziggurat', the rebuilt tower of Babel – symbol of defiance against God; and the temple of Marduk (Baal by his other name), the dragon-god, an evil spirit worshipped by self-torture and human sacrifice – surely the devil himself! The grand processional entrance to all this was through the Ishtar Gate. Covered with a swarm of monsters, including 337 snake-dragons (337 in Hebrew numerology means 'Sheol' or 'hell'), this was surely the gateway to this hell on earth, their captivity! No wonder when, by an absolute miracle, God released the Jews from Babylon seventy years later, their mouths were filled with laughter and their tongues with singing (Psalm 126)!

The evil spirit of Babylon...

Believers are warned from heaven in Revelation 18:4:

'*Come out of her* [Babylon], *my people, lest you share in her sins and lest you receive of her plagues. For her sins have reached to heaven, and God has remembered her iniquities.*'

Daniel, interpreting Nebuchadnezzar's dream of the statue, warns us that the evil spirit of Babylon would continue its activity after the fall of that ancient empire, inhabiting succeeding world kingdoms down to the present day. Only when Christ returns will the spirit of Babylon finally be overthrown (Daniel 2:33–34; Revelation 19:11–21). But what kingdoms do the feet of the image made of iron and clay represent today? Do they represent the kingdoms of Europe? Europe is not and has never been ten nations; but the Treaty of Rome has brought together an unlikely mixture of strength and weakness in the multitude of nations in the EU. Is this the end of the image which shall be broken by the return of Christ?

First the Medes and Persians inherited the evil spirit of Babylon when they captured the city in 539 BC. Overthrown by the Greeks in 331 BC, Alexander the Great had ten thousand men rebuild the temple of Marduk and ordered that daily sacrifices were to be made to Babylon's dragon-god until his premature death in 323 BC.

...is in Europe!

In 64 BC Rome overthrew the Greeks, lifting itself up as the new world empire. Daniel prophesied that this empire would continue in changing forms right until the return of Christ. Through the Romans the spirit of Babylon again struck the rebellious people of God, destroying their Temple in Jerusalem in AD 70 and scattering the Jews throughout the world in an exile which was to last until the miraculous re-establishment of Israel in 1948.

After the collapse of Imperial Rome, the Popes of Rome designated successive European kings as 'Holy Roman Emperors', political leaders of the Papal Holy Roman Empire. The title of Holy Roman Emperor was held by the Germanic Habsburg dynasty for hundreds of years; they also hold the title of 'King of Jerusalem' granted in perpetuity after the European Crusaders took Jerusalem from the Turks in 1061! They still carry the title today!

In 1898 Germany's Kaiser Wilhelm II visited the Holy Land in his capacity as 'King of Jerusalem', and one year later began excavations at the ancient site of Babylon. In 1913 he brought to Berlin the first pieces of the Gate and the Processional Way that are covered with the 337 snake-dragons – Babylon's entrance to hell on earth. Significantly, one year later Germany was at war with the world – which saw ten million dead in just four years!

By 1930 the entire Processional Way from Babylon was re-erected in Berlin. Was it co-incidence or fulfilment of prophecy that two years later Hitler took control as Chancellor of Germany (with the support of the churches)? Was it Babylon's snake-dragon god – the devil himself – that spoke through Hitler, announcing the 'final solution to the Jewish question', a solution which resulted in the holocaust of six million Jews in Europe? Not only that, but Hitler's World War II (1939–45) was truly hell on earth – resulting in fifty-five million dead worldwide.

Post-war Germany and Berlin were divided between the super-powers of East and West. Whilst East Berlin retained the Ishtar Gate, Babylon's symbol of hatred towards the Jews, West Germany moved into a period of grace. Chancellor Adenauer, a devout Christian and life-time opponent of Nazism, recognised the biblical truth that God will bless those who bless the Jews (Genesis 12:2–3). At a time when his own country lay in ruins, he offered war reparations to Israel – and the German post-war economic miracle began! All that changed when East and West Germany reunited in 1990.

Berlin, still with its Gate from Babylon, is once again the capital city; Chancellor Schroeder was in a hurry to move the seat of

German Government from Bonn in former West Germany to Berlin. President Clinton once called Berlin 'the heart of a united Europe'. What kind of a heart will it be? During World War II, when Hitler was fighting to establish his kingdom (Third Reich) on earth, he recorded his 'New Europe' policy for the control of post-war Europe: the Common European Currency, the Harmonisation of European Rates of Exchange, the European Economic Community, the European Agricultural Order etc. Despite his defeat, identical plans to his are being implemented in the European Union today! Do they originate in the prophecies of Daniel 2:41–44 – a divided kingdom in rebellion against God that will not remain united, destined to be swept away?

The spirit of Babylon through history

Nebuchadnezzar's empire was centred in Babylon – just a few kilometres outside today's Baghdad – but where was Nebuchadnezzar defeated? He was conquered by the Medes and Persians in Babylon. Where did the Greeks defeat the Medes and Persians? In Babylon. Where did the Romans defeat the Greeks? In Babylon. Where were the Romans defeated? This brings us up to prophecy in Europe today. The Roman Empire was at its height 2,000 years ago at the time of the New Testament. Who destroyed the Roman Empire? It was the Germanic tribes, this time not in Babylon, but in Europe! But instead of a complete defeat, the spirit of Rome remained alive. Suddenly the whole of Bible prophecy switches from Israel and Babylon – to Europe! This is very interesting for us in the twenty-first century.

After the time of Christ, the Roman Empire divided in two, with two capitals – Constantinople (Istanbul) and Rome – East and West – two legs! What happened? The power of the military empire went into the Church: one world Church centred in Rome, the Catholic Church; the other the Orthodox Church in Constantinople, the two legs of Daniel's image. The power of the Roman Empire is in the Church and in Europe today! Now, in the twenty-first century, we have the final empire, the feet, a continuation of the Roman Empire, based in Europe. The Bible says the feet are iron and clay – which don't mix! I believe the European Union is this fractured empire prophesied in the Bible – this European Union is such an unequal mixture that it cannot combine together as a cohesive union. There are so many divisions between the ten Eastern bloc countries and the fifteen Western European nations that the US refers to them as 'New Europe' and 'Old Europe' respectively. There is a strong move in Britain to resist the 'federalisation' and possibly come out altogether; the East European states have just been set free from the federal state of the Soviet Union, and the people don't want another one! So we will have twenty five nations united by only one thing – the fact that we are disunited.

The Mystery – Babylon the Great

'And I saw a woman sitting on a scarlet beast which was full of names of blasphemy, having seven heads and ten horns . . . And the ten horns which you saw on the beast, these will hate the harlot, make her desolate and naked, eat her flesh and burn her with fire.'
(Revelation 17:3, 16)

Jesus the Messiah, the Son of God, and His disciple John, who recorded for us the revelations of Jesus concerning the end times in which we are now living, were both born in Israel under the occupation of the European Roman Empire. Interestingly Greek is the language of the New Testament. It was also a language common in Israel at the time of Christ. The inscription on the cross of Christ was written in Latin, Greek, and Aramaic! I believe the woman John wrote about in Revelation 17 is the Europa of Greek mythology.

Greek mythology – Europe, Babylon and the beast

Growing up under European Greek-Roman culture, Jesus and John would have known of the myths of the Greek-Roman gods, including the one famously called 'The Rape of Europe' which tells how the continent was named. When Jesus revealed to John the woman of Revelation 17, sitting upon a scarlet beast with many horns, was He speaking of Europe today? And why was this woman called 'Mystery **Babylon** the Great'? And who does the powerful beast with horns represent?

In mythology Zeus, the father of the gods, seeing a beautiful woman, Europa (or Europe) on the shores of the Middle East, disguised himself as a bull with crescent horns and raped her. The symbol for the father of the Middle East pagan gods (Baal, as we know him from archaeology and from the Bible, Zeus-Jupiter as we know him from Greek-Roman culture) was a **bull** with great **crescent** horns! And the ruling god of ancient **Babylon** and the Middle East was the **moon** god, depicted as a bull with crescent horns, or simply as the crescent moon! I believe Allah is this same moon god that Muhammad chose to worship – the same crescent moon is the universal symbol of Islam, on its mosques and flags everywhere today!

Violent struggle in history

Look at history: from the beginning Islam has struggled with Europe. First, the incursions of Islam into Europe through Turkey, the Balkans, Spain and France – to overwhelm Europe by war, then the European Crusader invasions into the Bible Land of Israel, to wrest control of the Land from Islam.

Oil makes Moslem Middle East desirable

'The Great Game' is the name given to the competition played out between European countries (including America and Russia) for economic and political control of the Middle and Far East. Originally it was the wealth of India which made control of the Far East the greatest prize; but since the invention of the internal combustion engine and the discovery of vast oil reserves ('black gold'), the nations of Islam became politically and economically the most desirable on earth.

During World War I, Europe (France and UK versus Germany, Austria and Turkey) fought over the Middle East. Britain and France dismantled the Ottoman-Turkish Empire which controlled large parts of the Middle East and Eastern Europe from the fourteenth to the twentieth centuries, and parcelled out today's Arab countries – centred on oil fields and other major strategic interests.

In 1917, when the French and the British were driving the occupying Moslem Turks (and Germans) out of Israel and Jerusalem and the surrounding areas, the British government cut deals with both Jews and Arabs to gain maximum support, laying the foundation of today's conflicts. Britain promised: first to the Jews through Lord Balfour to 'view with favour the establishment in Palestine of a national home for the Jewish people', and second to the Moslem Arabs, through the British Commissioner in Egypt, to recognise and support the independence of the Arabs from the Turks.

This violent union of Europe and the lands of Islam, begun in World War I, took another twist in World War II. On 28th November 1941 the Moslem Grand Mufti of Jerusalem met with Hitler to make a covenant: the Arabs would give their support to Hitler's war on condition that, after eradicating the Jews in Europe, Hitler would then eradicate the Jewish National Homeland.

Since World War II, the 'union' between Islam and Europe has continued – a peaceful immigration of Europe has taken place. Migrant workers and refugees have been welcomed in. At the beginning of the twenty-first century, Germany had three million Moslem Turks; France had five million North African Moslems, and Britain had two million Moslems from her former colonies and elsewhere. Islam is the second largest, and fastest, growing religion in Britain today. Europe has been penetrated extensively; Islam welcomed liberally, land donated freely for her mosques and schools. And whilst European culture is suppressed in Islamic countries and the practise of the Christian faith forbidden by law, in our European countries we are afraid to offend Islam. Our European Christian leaders make loving, interfaith overtures towards the Babylonian moon god, Allah, to recognise him as another, equal revelation of the God of the Bible.

Europe, Islam – and Israel?

When we read in Ezekiel 38–39 about the nations that come
against Israel in the last days, we easily identify the Moslem nations
– Persia (Iran / Iraq), Ethiopia, Libya. Are the other countries
European? Could Gomer be Germany as some commentators
suggest? Gog, the land of Magog, the leading nation against Israel,
is traditionally Russia, which is also part of the European land-
mass. But I was shocked to find that Britain has an ancient tradition
that Gog and Magog are the gods of London. Their effigies can be
found in London's Guildhall, and models have been paraded in
the Lord Mayor's annual procession for nearly six hundred years,
and still are today! Also we should not forget that, whilst Bible-
believing America is still seen to be Israel's friend, she was
originally settled mainly by Europeans.

The Bible says that ultimately *all* the nations of the earth will be
gathered against Jerusalem in battle, and at that time the Lord
Himself will return (Zechariah 14:2–4).

The Seat of Satan – in Europe

'To the angel of the church in Pergamos write ... "I know your works, and where you dwell, where Satan's throne is. And you hold fast to My name, and did not deny My faith even in the days in which Antipas was My faithful martyr, who was killed among you, where Satan dwells."'

(Revelation 2:12–13)

The gigantic 'Altar of Pergamon' or Pergamos dominates Germany's Pergamon Museum in former East Berlin. Originally sited in Asia Minor, the Temple at Pergamon with its altar was the centre of Emperor worship; the price of refusal to acknowledge the Roman Emperor as God – ritual murder on the altar! Revelation 2:13 calls it 'Satan's Seat' or 'The Throne of Satan', and records that here Antipas was martyred for his unswerving faith in Christ. German archaeologist Carl Humann discovered the altar in the late 1800s and carefully shipped every stone to Berlin. In 1902 Kaiser (Emperor) Wilhelm II celebrated its erection in Berlin as the 'proudest monument to his reign' – with an extravagant festival to the pagan gods!

It is significant that within a short time of this the history of Germany was to be dominated by a sequence of events which could only be attributed to satanic control. Following the Welsh Revival of 1904 which, although known worldwide, was to affect only part of Britain, came the outpouring of the Holy Spirit in

1908. Almost simultaneously in an Anglican Church in Monk Weirmouth in the UK, in Azusa Street in Los Angeles, USA, and soon afterwards in Kassel in Germany, people gathering together in prayer and worship began speaking in unknown tongues! This was the beginning of the worldwide Pentecostal outpouring of God's Spirit – marked by this phenomena known as 'speaking in tongues' just as on the day of Pentecost in Acts 2.

Unfortunately Germany became the principal seat of rejection of this new move which was clearly from God. At a meeting of the Evangelical Alliance of Germany, in Berlin, the evangelical churches issued what is known as the 1909 Berlin Declaration with the following conclusions:

> 'The so-called Pentecostal Movement is not from above, but from below ... Demons are at work in it and, led with cunning by Satan, lies are mixed together with truth in order to lead the children of God astray ... Neither the personal faithfulness and devotion of some individual leading brethren, nor the healings, tongues and prophecy etc. which accompany this movement can change our conviction that this movement is from below ... the spirit in this movement produces neither spiritual nor physical works of power, but it is a false spirit. It has exposed itself as such ... '

Yet God promised in His Word that He would pour out His Spirit on all flesh (Joel 2:28; Acts 2:17) – not just the light showers of the first Pentecost, but the heavy rain that brings in the last abundant harvest of souls (Joel 2:23–24) *'before the coming of the great and awesome day of the* LORD*'* (Joel 2:31; Acts 2:20).

Can one be surprised that by the 1920s, the German Church had become the seat of 'modern biblical criticism' and 'liberal theology', questioning the truth of Holy Scripture, undermining the very foundations of faith worldwide!? Just as the move of God's Spirit went worldwide, so did this diabolical lie. The idea was promoted that the Bible was not the inspired Word of God, only a 'history' story-book, a collection of beautiful poetry and exciting myths, especially the 'myth of God-incarnate' – the absolute rejection of who Christ Jesus really is. God was stripped of His divinity, His Word stripped of authority – and the Jewish people of their irrevocable election and calling. With the long European Catholic and Protestant tradition of anti-semitism (hatred of Jews as 'God-killers'), this led easily to Hitler's Holocaust of the Jews – with almost no protest but rather support from the leadership of the Church. (If you have sometimes wondered why it is so hard for you to believe wholeheartedly, it is probably the subversive and pervasive influence of this liberal heritage. We must repent and choose to believe.)

Hitler was so impressed by the Pergamon Altar in Berlin that in 1934 he commissioned a grand reproduction to be made for his Nazi rallies in Nuremberg. Here, from *'Satan's Throne'*, he decreed death to the Jews and all those not possessing Aryan blood or confessing the Aryan faith. Mainstream churches officially supported Hitler, but many Germans – from all denominations – paid with their lives for holding fast to their faith in Christ and for sheltering Jews during the ensuing Nazi persecution (Revelation 2:13).

In recent years, led by the new Charismatic Churches, there were many separate repentances for the 1909 Berlin Declaration, notably at the March for Jesus in Berlin in 1994. However, in 1996 the Berlin Declaration, which had been a spiritual Berlin Wall dividing believers in Germany, fell! After many years of heart-searching, the German Evangelical Alliance together with the Union of Free Pentecostal Churches signed a joint declaration of reconciliation – called the Kassel Declaration – agreeing to pray together for revival and to work together in evangelism.

Since the collapse of the physical Berlin Wall, the re-united city has been rebuilt and prepared to take its place as the historical heart of Germany and the centre of a united Europe. In April 1999, the Reichstag building, made famous by Hitler – destroyed in 1945 and now completely rebuilt – was officially opened, and in September 1999 the German Government moved from Bonn back to Berlin and the Reichstag. For the first time in fifty years the

German Government returned to its place – where the 'Seat of Satan' is.

What is the spiritual significance? Why has this move taken place at this time of the creation of a single European State? Will this spirit dominate Europe? Will there be pressure for the European Parliament with its operation split between Strasbourg and Brussels to be re-located in one of the many re-furbished and vacant historical buildings in Berlin, where the 'Seat of Satan' is?

Key dates in the spiritual history of Germany

1867	Berlin becomes capital of German Confederation
1902	Pergamon's Altar (Satan's Seat) erected in Berlin – Kaiser Wilhelm II celebrates as the highest achievement of his reign with a pagan festival to the gods!
1908	Simultaneous outpouring of the Holy Spirit in Britain and America
1909	'Berlin Declaration' attributes the Pentecostal movement to the devil!
1913	First pieces of Babylon's 'Gateway to Hell' brought to Berlin
1914	Germany invades Belgium, World War I begins – ten million die
1920s	Germany, the seat of modern liberal theology
1930	Babylon's entire Gateway and Processional Way erected in Berlin
1934	Hitler orders reproduction of Pergamon's Altar (Satan's Throne) for his Nazi rallies in Nuremberg
1939–45	World War II – fifty-five million dead; holocaust of Europe's Jews – six million die
1945	Hitler defeated; dismantled pieces of Pergamon Altar carried away as booty to Leningrad
1947	'Marshall Plan' sets a united Europe in motion
1958	At the request of the Germans, Khrushchev sends the Pergamon Altar back

1959   Pergamon Altar re-erected in the Pergamon Museum,
        East Berlin

1999   Germany's capital again in Berlin; Europe's Prime
        Ministers meet in Berlin, described by President
        Clinton as the 'heart of a united Europe'

God Banned from Europe!

The Treaty of Lisbon was signed by the European Union member states in 2007 and entered into force in December 2009. It amends the 1992 'Treaty on European Union' and the original 'Treaty Establishing the European Community' from 1957. Prominent changes include the creation of President of the European Council and a High Representative of the Union for Foreign Affairs and Security Policy. Opponents to the Treaty see it as part of a federalist agenda that threatens national sovereignty.

Negotiations to modify the EU began in 2001, resulting first in the European Constitution, which was rejected in referenda by French and Dutch voters in 2005.

Most European leaders acknowledge, however, that the Lisbon Treaty preserves the main substance of the rejected Constitution. In 2007, the former French president Valery Giscard d'Estaing, writing in *The Independent* newspaper in Britain, said: 'In the Treaty of Lisbon, the tools are largely the same. Only the order in which they are arranged in the tool-box has been changed.' He went on to say that references to the Constitution have been removed 'above all to head off any threat of referenda by avoiding any form of constitutional vocabulary'. He continued: 'When the day comes that men and women with sweeping ambitions for Europe decide to make use of this treaty, they will be able to rekindle from the ashes of today the flame of a United Europe.'

The Constitution was an attempt to unite 450 million people from the then twenty-five states (the EU in 2009 has twenty-seven states), embracing all major strands of European culture under one supreme legal document – without a mention of God!

In its Preamble (that is the introduction to and the founding influence behind the Constitution), the Constitution named Greek and Roman civilisations as the formative traditions of Europe – not Christianity! Does this identify Europe as the successor to the Babylonian/Medo-Persian/Greek/Roman empires of Daniel 2 and with the feet of the statue that will be smashed by Christ's return?

Valery Giscard d'Estaing, former French President and humanist, and President of the committee which drew up the draft, rejected the mention of God, but had these words included in the Preamble:

> '... Europe is a continent that has brought forth civilisation ... its inhabitants, arriving in successive waves since the beginning of time, have gradually developed over the centuries the values that are the foundation of humanism: equality of all humans, liberty, respect for reason ... '

The decision to ban God from the Constitution was taken – as always in Europe – behind closed doors, by an unelected group of thirteen, and was based on a paper entitled *'Let's Leave God Out of This'*, drafted by Convention Member and hardline socialist Joseph Borrell Fontelles. The decision was welcomed by Turkey, who together with Europe's fourteen million Moslems, resents the EU as a predominantly 'Christian club'.

Official EU thinking is that religion/faith is something cultural or national, like the clothes you wear, the food you eat, the language you speak, the colour you are – just something inherited from the society or group you were born into. In mainland Europe this might be Catholic or Lutheran; in Britain – Anglican, Catholic or Free Church; in Eastern Europe – Orthodoxy, indeed any religion found within your geographical region. Even elements of wicca or witchcraft are given recognition as being our pure ancestral pagan roots! And to promote racial harmony, schools and media teach and inform about the religions of those minority cultures that now live among us.

The official position is that you are, by chance, born into a particular culture or religion, and that all cultures, religions and philosophies are equal, and all can be freely practised, mixed, or rejected – except pure faith in Jesus Christ. Both the EU and national governments are increasingly passing laws to restrict/prohibit the activities of those groups and churches who believe and preach the Gospel, that there is only *one* God, and only *one* way to salvation, through God's *only* Son Jesus Christ.

Adrian Hilton writing in *Intelligence Digest* No. 15 (November 2004) comments about the Constitution:

> 'The constitution is itself rigorously secular, all reference to God (Christianity) having been removed, leaving only the values of Humanism and Enlightenment.'

For two hundred and fifty years the European 'Enlightenment' movement has delighted in criticising faith in the God of the Bible as dark unreason, and has exalted humanism and human reason above God as the highest goal of civilised society. Now, in the Preamble of the Constitution, godless humanism and human reason undergird the whole Constitution of Europe!

Yes, the EU likes to say that it is a community of values. In fact many of its values have sprung from its former Christian faith, but many are being eroded by godlessness. A code of 'Human Rights' replaces the Ten Commandments of the Word of God. Romans 1:21–32 warns that when men fail to honour God – though they believe themselves to be wise and reasonable – their hearts in fact become darkened and they become fools; when men call God a liar, and honour created man rather than the Creator, they open themselves to every vile and perverse thing. God's values are lost.

'The optimism of the eighteenth-century Enlightenment can be pardoned for its belief in reason,' says German intercessor for Europe, Ortwin Schweitzer.

> 'But it is unforgivable to offer this optimistic faith [in reason] to a Europe that has gone through two World Wars and the Holocaust, despite placing reason on the throne in every area. This is why, after the horror of the Third Reich, the fathers of the German Constitution included God in it. They felt only people who were guided by pleasing God and living accordingly, could ensure peace and liberty in Europe.'

The fact that there are several dominant religions in Europe – and likely to be more in the future – is an argument cited for leaving the word 'Christian' out of the Preamble and the Constitution – a decision opposed by EU-member Poland, but welcomed by Moslem Turkey.

Historically, from the Crusades to the Inquisition, to the Holocaust, European Christianity is guilty. But the origin of these crimes cannot be found in the teachings of Jesus Christ, only in sinful man himself. Following Muhammad's own example recorded in the Koran, Islam's goal is to build a god-state, the House of Islam, to gain the predominance of power everywhere, by any means, including deceit (peace treaties that are made only to be broken at the right time) and *jihad* (terror and war). When Turkey finally joins the EU it will be the most powerful member state by reason of its large youthful population, toppling France and Germany from their place of leadership.

Ortwin Schweitzer (German intercessor for Europe) stated:

> 'Coming generations may wish the fathers of the European Constitution had named the Judeo-Christian tradition as formative for Europe so that it would be clear that Europe cannot be a House of Islam. Today we are still in the phase of tolerance, with Moslems in the minority. However, through terrorism, we are noticing the lava bubbling beneath our

feet ... By omitting the Judeo-Christian name of God as the basis of our culture, the Preamble to the Constitution opens the door for Islam's vision of building Europe into a House of Islam. Europe may be ruined one day because of its idea of tolerance, of which it is so proud, by those who do not share this definition of tolerance but know how to use it to reach their goals.'

CHAPTER 9

Will Islam Rule Europe?

It is commonly said in the West that there are three peoples of the 'Book': the Jews who believe the Old Testament, the Christians who believe in the entire Bible, and the Moslems with their Koran. But Allah is not our God – we worship the God of Abraham, Isaac and Jacob, while they believe themselves to be the spiritual descendants of Abraham's son by Hagar, Ishmael. Look at Islamic symbols – the crescent on the mosques and on the flags of the Moslems is in the shape of the horns of a bull! Is this Baal, the bull god of the Old Testament? Then when you compare this with the symbolism from Revelation 17, the Rape of Europe by the beast, the beast is significant because of its horns!

Militant Moslem fanaticism is threatening world stability. In Israel it is not just a question of the conflict being over territory as many imagine, the fact is the Moslems intend to destroy Israel totally. Since the militant Islamic Hamas party won the demo-cratic election to govern the Palestinians, they have not renounced terror, nor their determination to refuse to accept the existence of the State of Israel. Their constitution declares the total destruction of Israel. They not only want the 'right of return' – Jerusalem and the so-called 'occupied' territories – they will not rest until every Jew is massacred or out of the Land. It is in their charter.

After Israel, the next enemy is the Church. Militants hate the Cross; they hate every Christian symbol. Even now, all over the world, wherever they see Christian symbols, they are building mosques to show the ascendancy of Islam over the Christian faith. Saudi Arabia has been building mosques worldwide, even where there are few Moslems, yet in Saudi Arabia you can be jailed for having a Bible and no churches can be built there. When the city of Rome allowed the building of a mosque near the Vatican, Saudi press saw this as surrender to Islam! The West may practise interfaith and invite leading imams into Christian Cathedrals and shrines, but the Islamic cities of Mecca and Medina are forbidden to anyone who does not practise Islam.

The Koran teaches that the world must be taken for Islam by *jihad*, territorially (Sura 2:187, 189, 190–194, 216, 217; 4:91, 94–96; 5:37; 8:12–16, 39, 40, 57, 65, 67; 9:5, 14, 23, 29, 30, 41, 73, 112, 124; 47:4–7 and many others).

Islam divides the world into two parts – the House of Islam (those at peace with God – Moslems) and the House of War (non-Moslems – infidels). If you are not a Moslem, you may be the target of *jihad* or Holy War. If militant Moslems gain control in your country, you will be subjected to Islamic (Shariah) law – look at Saudi Arabia, Iran, Afghanistan, Pakistan, Northern Nigeria and now Iraq . . . (the site of the original Babylon).

Jihad in Israel . . .

There is a historical reason why Jerusalem is the focal point of Islamic Jihad: the whole of the Holy Land came into 'the House of Islam' when Jerusalem was captured by Muhammad's successor, Caliph Omar in AD 638. After Mecca and Medina, Jerusalem became the third most holy Moslem site. Any territory that has once been conquered by Islam must forever remain Moslem – and any territory subsequently lost must be re-taken (whether Israel – or Europe). To the Moslem, Allah could not allow the Jews to take even part of the Holy Land in 1948. Moslems even say that the Jewish people never possessed the land and never had a Temple there! Western intellectuals can laugh and say no intelligent person would ever swallow this, but a lie often repeated gains credibility.

Jihad in Europe...

In 1453 Constantinople, for a thousand years the Christian capital of the Eastern Roman Empire and known as the 'second Rome', fell to Mehmed II, ruler of the Ottoman Turks. As the result of this strategic conquest, Mehmed was viewed by Islam as heir to the Roman Emperors, rightful ruler of Europe and of Christianity, Judaism and Islam (*BBC History* magazine, June 2002). As a sign of perpetual submission to Islam, the proudest cathedral of Eastern Christianity, Santa Sofia, in Constantinople (modern Istanbul), became a mosque.

Turkey's possible inclusion in the EU has a serious spiritual, political and territorial impact because Islam lays claims to all Europe. In May 2002 the European Union held a meeting in Seville, Spain, to deal with the issue of refugees in Europe. It was picketed by Moslem refugees claiming the right to live in Europe – based on earlier conquests by Islam (Seville was held for three centuries from AD 711). Seville was, historically, the Moslem capital of Western Europe.

The Moslem Manifesto for Great Britain, published in London in June 1990, clearly sets the Moslem agenda. Here are some statements made:

- In their role as a colonial power [i.e. until the end of World War II] the British used the modernists [i.e. moderates within Islam] to deflect and abort Moslem opposition to their rule; they promoted an emasculated form of Islam from which the component of *jihad* was subtracted. They are now attempting to do the same in dealing with Moslems living in Britain.
- Every Moslem should seek to develop an identity in terms of the goals of Islam and participate in the struggle of the global Islamic movement towards these goals.
- *Jihad* is a basic requirement of Islam, and living in Britain or having British nationality by birth or naturalisation does not absolve the Moslem from his or her duty to participate in *jihad*; this participation can be active service in armed

struggle abroad and/or the provision of material and moral support to those engaged in such struggle anywhere in the world.

Our only hope is Christ!

World destabilisation, fear and anxiety, and a genuine desire for world peace make many Christians lean favourably towards inter-faith, letting-go of one's own convictions, approving the convictions of others. Many share the unbiblical belief of the fourteenth Dalai Lama: 'The core of all religions is the same.' But the Bible warns that if you do not receive the truth about your salvation, you will receive a strong delusion instead and believe what is actually a lie (2 Thessalonians 2:10–11). But if your faith in Jesus is firm, you cannot, you will not, let Him go! He is your only hope, now and for eternity.

The Good News for humanity is:

> *'God so loved the world that He gave His only begotten Son, that whoever believes in Him should not perish but have everlasting life.'*
>
> (John 3:16)

Our only hope for the future is in Jesus Christ!

God's Answer!

I began working in Russia forty years ago because I saw the pain and the suffering in the people, but what I see in Europe renews that feeling – we are in a desperate, final spiritual fight for the nations!

We read in Exodus 3:1 that Moses was keeping the sheep of his father-in-law and took them to the back of the desert, to the mountain of God, to Horeb. It is as if the Holy Spirit is saying, 'Look at Moses, he's a shepherd, a pastor, he's eighty years old, a man who has gone through many experiences, born as a slave, adopted into the king's palace, became a murderer, then fled the country – and now he's spent more than forty years in a desert, how can God use him?'

We all come from different experiences in life. One of the best evangelists I know, who today preaches in all the prisons in the Far East Russia, was converted in one of my meetings in a Siberian prison.

What God is saying here in Exodus is a challenge to you and me, to every pastor, evangelist and leader, whoever you are, however long you have been preaching the Gospel. We see Moses as the pastor-shepherd, and yet now after forty years' experience, he finds himself in a desert. But God has not forgotten this man and after eighty years of preparation, now God begins to deal with him in a new way – something powerful is about to happen in the life of Moses. The Angel of the Lord appears in a flame of fire, out of the midst of a bush – and Moses turns aside to see what is happening.

I believe there comes a time in our lives when, however long we have been serving God, God wants to challenge us and attract our attention because He wants to do something new, something more powerful through us. It is easy to become so involved in the shepherding that we feel that this is our total future. Often, even in spiritual things, they follow a predictable pattern. God gives a special vision, a revelation to a man; this becomes shared, then a committee takes over, this then becomes a denomination. So, within two generations the fire has gone and the whole thing is mired in the formality of an organisational structure. Not often do you see the fire of God's vision in an organisation; as with Moses, experiencing the fire comes through a direct and personal contact with God. This is the whole background to the Bible – Moses, Abraham, David, Elijah ... men, not denominations, men with a personal experience which comes through a direct, life-changing experience with God.

I know that on at least two occasions God has had to bring me to a complete stop rather forcefully – once it was incarceration in a communist prison, but more recently, still quite dramatically – in order to change my direction. Even now I know that God wants to make a new beginning in *my* life – I'm older than most of you – but God is challenging me, at my age, because He wants to begin something new. He's calling me to come aside, to look again at the fire, until a new motivation and a new passion burn within me.

One hundred years ago in Britain we had the Welsh Revival. It reached many – over 100,000 came to Christ. But today everywhere I go, in England, in Europe, I find a real desperate cry for another revival fire to touch our people. Where has that fire of revival gone? Did it survive two generations, or less? Secularism has taken over; a whole generation has grown up that knows nothing about God or the Bible. Even believers are saying that we are living in a post-Christian period and in the new Europe there are possibly fewer than 1% real baptised believers.

Today many of us sing, 'These are the days of Elijah', but my question is: where is Elijah today? We need to pray that God will again speak to a man like Moses, or Elijah.

Today, if God does not touch the existing pastors, the leaders, with a new fire, there is no hope for our people – unless He can find another Moses out in the desert – we are in a deep spiritual wilderness!

We need an awakening that will touch and will shake our nation that will bring real conviction of sin to the unbeliever. But this means we need more of the power of God *in us*! Only the Holy Spirit can bring that conviction, not organisation. In Exodus 3, I find Moses as the shepherd-pastor – he knew God, he already had an experience with Him, he grew up belonging to the people of God. But then the Lord appeared to him in a new way, in the fire! We need the Lord to appear to us like this and call us again! We need a new fire in our lives!

Elijah was a man *just* like us with the same emotions (James 5:17). But he had such a powerful relationship with God that when he called upon Him, God answered – by fire! The thing that changed Moses even after eighty years' experience with God was turning aside to meet Him personally and allowing Him to speak. And what did God say first?

> *'I have surely seen the oppression of My people . . . and have heard their cry because of their taskmasters, for I know their sorrows. So I have come down to deliver them . . . '*
>
> (Exodus 3:7–8)

I don't know how many years you have been in ministry, in leadership, how long you have known God, but I believe passionately that because of the sorrow, the suffering, the affliction of the people, God wants to answer their cry now!

Christian leaders, can't you see the emptiness in people's eyes? Why are our best young people turning to drugs, to binge drinking? Just for the fun of it? Or is it because of the emptiness, the loneliness and despair of a life without Christ? No politician today has the real answer to the ills of our modern, Western society. The root cause is not social deprivation or poverty, but a national rejection of God. Maybe the 'Church' does not have the answer, but the 'Word of God' does!

Right now, God **wants** to send a fresh outpouring of the Holy Spirit over the nations in Europe, but to do this He needs to call us as motivated believers aside, to talk to us strongly, to attract our attention in a new way. We need a *renewed* fire, but an 'old-time' revival, we need a *new* power, but the 'real' God. Will you be the one whom He will call again, through the fire of the Holy Spirit?

The reason so much of the so-called 'Church' in Europe is sick, is that it does not know or experience the **real** power of God. Its faith is based, not on the demonstration of God's power, but on doctrines and teachings of men, social programmes, human-aid, even on false manifestations which are not the real power of God. But we **need** to demonstrate the true power of a loving God to save, to heal, to deliver, and to give *new* life.

Today we are in a desperate, final spiritual fight for the nations! Complacency, godlessness, humanism, money, political power, world control, antichrist, Islam, all are fighting to take control. Do you really believe we **can** have power with God and with man to deliver a whole nation from evil as Moses did? Do you believe in a demonstration of the Spirit's power great enough to convert a whole nation in one day as Elijah did? If we say it can't be done, do we **really** know God, do we **really** know His power? This is the challenge, but if we don't do something to win them now – the devil will!

God Has a Vision – for Europe!

I have a vision in my soul – Eurovision – a vision of Europe won for Christ. This vision is God's vision, God's desire – to see His power, His glory in Europe, and I will not rest until God fulfils this vision that He has put within my soul.

But this is only the beginning of what God wants to do. When I see what God actually will do in Europe – this burns in my soul.

God had a vision when He created the world, and the Bible says that when God spoke, the vision came to life! A world with no sin, suffering, hunger, disease, pain or death. God in heaven had a glorious vision of a beautiful, perfect world, where man lived in harmony with man and in communion with God. When God began to create the earth, it was to fulfil this vision He already had. When He looked at the nations of Europe – the Middle East – Russia – Africa – Asia – America – He saw a glorious creation, filled with His glory and power!

Then the devil came and ruined God's dream. He brought disobedience, fear, sin and death – all the things that distress and disturb our world came from Satan when he sowed that first seed of doubt, 'Did God say?'

But God had another vision, ready, in anticipation of Satan's action! This was that He would send His Son into the world, that Jesus, by His power and authority, by His death and resurrection, would break the power of Satan, set men free – a vision of men and women saved from sin, delivered from sickness, filled with the

Holy Ghost – waiting for the final redemption, when God will restore the earth to its first glory! For this reason the Bible speaking of Jesus refers to Him as, *'the Lamb slain from the foundation of the world'* (Revelation 13:8). So the way of redemption was prepared before sin came!

If you could catch the glory and the power of this vision that God has within His heart today, it would change your life, your church, your nation.

I burn with a vision for Europe, not because it is my vision, but because it is God's heart, God's desire, and God will not rest until that vision becomes fact.

For thirty years under communism I preached in Eastern Europe – it was so hard with all the barriers, all the problems of the Iron Curtain, and with the churches being underground (illegal – hidden), because of persecution. Then God gave me a vision that the borders would open, that the Iron Curtain would be melted by the power of the Holy Spirit. God challenged me to hold a prophetic conference in West Germany, and to believe for hundreds to come from the East, across the borders. In 1988 and again in 1989, thousands of Westerners attended, and each time six hundred delegates came from the East, by a miracle, through the Iron Curtain! I stood almost alone at that time – little money, few workers – I only had the Holy Spirit. But my vision was of God and His glory, and in 1989, just days after the end of the second East-West Conference, the vision and the prophecy were fulfilled and the Iron Curtain came down!

When God gave me this vision that He would break the Iron Curtain, He showed me that the power of the Holy Spirit would then sweep across the whole of Europe from East to West. So I followed the East Europeans and the Russians back into their own countries. Since 1989 so much of prophecy has been fulfilled! We have seen revival fire fall in Odessa, Ukraine, in 1992 – a move of the Holy Spirit that is still sweeping the whole of the former Soviet Union today. Again in 1992, I was the first evangelist ever to take the big Dynamo Stadium in Kiev! Two students, who were my interpreters then, are pastors of the biggest churches in Kiev today;

one has the largest church in all Europe – over 25,000! Another young man, who now pastors the largest church in South Ukraine, said, 'Miracles became very strong in Ukraine after David Hathaway's crusade in Kiev in 1992. Until then it had been hard, but from that point it was a breakthrough and it became very simple.'

Then God showed me that I must go to the far side of Russia, to Siberia and the Far East, and that the revival that would come into Europe would come from there. One young man, who evangelised with me in Siberia in 1994, now pastors the largest Messianic congregation in Europe – in Kiev! And many of the churches in Ukraine who have worked with me are already evangelising in Europe – especially amongst the Russian émigrés in Germany, Spain and Portugal.

Europe is the least evangelised continent in the world. Yes, there is still much religion, but God wants to set Europe on fire by His Holy Spirit. Since 1984, even when still under communism, I was holding crusades in all of Eastern Europe and, since 1991, in the former Soviet Union. We've seen hundreds of thousands accept Christ, and many thousands of miracles of healing! In 2002 I was preaching in the city of Perm. The evangelism was in a large indoor sports stadium seating 6,000, but as I left the city I was in a rebellious mood. I had seen the statistics published earlier by a Swedish organisation – that in Russia only a half of one percent of Russians were baptised (evangelical) believers.

As I flew out of that city on my way to our big Conference in Jerusalem I was so rebellious, complaining to the Lord all the way to Moscow that if I could not do any better I would not return to Russia but evangelise somewhere else. But by the time we arrived in Moscow airport with my team – God had put an idea in my head. I asked my TV Director if it was possible to broadcast the whole crusade live on the local TV channels to the whole city. 'Of course,' he replied, 'the system was set up in the whole of Russia for the purpose of communist propaganda.'

Six months later we were back in Russia and began the most amazing system of evangelism – broadcasting the whole crusade services live on the local TV channels not just to the city, but to the whole region. Now not just 6,000 but the whole region could participate – up to five million people – we broadcast the music, Gospel message, call to repentance, prayer for the sick – and God answered by fire! Miracles happened live on air – people watching at home were saved, healed, and came into the crusade services to report the miracles happening! This was the biggest breakthrough – but we did not stop there. By the following Easter we had bought special satellite equipment to enable us to link regions right across Russia. Still broadcasting on the ordinary TV as Russians outside of Moscow and St Petersburg don't have satellite TV, but linking the twenty or more broadcasting stations with a satellite dish, we reached over ten million that first Easter!

Now in December 2005 I was on my way back from a pioneer crusade in Kudimkar, Russia – yes, preaching in the open air in a blizzard, minus 15°C – and met with the pastors in a Russian city called Perm. After warming up in a typical Russian 'banya' at the pastor's home and enjoying the meal his wife provided we discussed how we could reach all Russia with the Gospel!

Again the Holy Spirit provided the miraculous inspiration – in 2005 Russia set up the 'free phone' or 0800 system where we set up a number of telephone lines (and pay for them), but callers from anywhere in Russia can call us free of charge. (This is important because few Russians have telephones in their homes – they have to use public ones which are expensive and they need the money to buy bread.) Now we had the idea – in January 2006 at the Russian Orthodox Christmas when there are no restrictions on religious programmes, we would simultaneously hold crusades in two cities and broadcast to two regions on the four most popular channels, then setting up banks of free phone lines in each church and running the phone numbers on the TV screens constantly, make personal contact with the millions watching!

We set it up – advertised the broadcasts on TV, in newspapers, on radio, in the buses, posters on billboards – then held the meetings and broadcast them live!

The response was about two hundred times greater than we had anticipated. Literally thousands of people, who had never been able to do anything like this before, called the counsellors in the churches. They estimated that over six million people watched the broadcast Crusade meetings live during those two days! None of us had anticipated the response and we did not have enough phones or counsellors. But – the system worked – and has proved that we can reach all Russia.

Today we are following through with this system – improving all the time – now we can reach every village, every home, set up cell groups and house churches all over Russia!

Because we believe that this is the call and commission from God, we are doing this right now. Russia is divided into seven major regions and we can reach all Russia in three years. We did not wait – the cost is enormous – the advertising, the crusades, the phone calls are expensive. But our God is able! The Bible says that *'faith* [or even vision] *without works is dead'* (James 2:26).

We have begun – and God has called us not only to begin, but to finish the work – the vision came from God, and He will do it. All I have to do is obey Him!

The day of visions is almost at an end. This is the day of action. Yes, I have a vision; this is why the Holy Spirit burns in my soul. But God is challenging Europe. God is putting a new power in the Church. In Numbers 27, Moses says this to God,

> ' *"Let the* LORD *... set a man over the congregation..."*
> *And the* LORD *said to Moses: "Take Joshua the son of Nun with you, a man in whom is the Spirit..."* '
>
> (Numbers 27:16, 18)

Joshua was already a man full of the Spirit!

I have a message for you: God has already chosen men; God has already put His power within them! There is no waiting. God says, 'There are men now, men from your nation, and I have already put My power in them!' We pray for revival, we wait for revival, and say, 'If I had the power I would preach, if I had the anointing I would heal the sick, I would raise the dead.' But God says, 'The men I have chosen have the power already, at this moment, within them!' Today! Now! The Holy Ghost is here! So often we are waiting for the Holy Spirit, for God's power to move. But I ask this question, is there any power greater than that which raised Jesus from the dead, that fell on the day of Pentecost, and that has fallen on you? There is no power other than the Holy Spirit! If only we would get the vision of the power that has already been given to us who have received the Holy Spirit! Take the anointing by faith and go out and do it now!

Don't talk to me only about a vision for the future. The vision is for now, today! I have the power – Pentecost fell on me – I have the glory of God – and so do you! The glory of God is here – just open your eyes and see! Get the vision. Mix your vision with faith. Act! Nothing is impossible!

Read Ezekiel 12:22 where God says:

> ' . . . what is this proverb that you people have . . . which says, "The days are prolonged, and every vision fails"?'

But, God says:

> 'I will lay this proverb to rest, and they shall no more use it . . . The days are at hand, and the fulfilment of every vision.'
>
> (Ezekiel 12:23)

God is saying, in your church, in your nation, you are saying the prophet is prophesying about something that cannot happen for a long time, that Europe is not yet ready, it's impossible. But He answers in verse 28:

> 'None of My words will be postponed any more, but the word which I speak will be done.'

We have seen this begin to happen in Ukraine, in Russia. But God says, 'Speak to the whole of Europe, none of My promises will delay any more. Everything I have promised – everything I have written, everything in the Book – all that you have believed for – is going to happen! The word which I have spoken shall be done. The day of visions is ended, now is the day of action!'

I speak on the authority of the Word of God to the whole of Europe. We must declare the power of God – because God has spoken! Today Europe is in spiritual bondage. But God wants to demonstrate His power in Europe. For over fifty years I have a vision of revival that burns in my soul. God will work greater miracles than Europe has ever seen in its entire history.

What is God's Strategy?

Remember that God has always had a clear plan and strategy in everything He does. From creation to salvation, nothing has happened in heaven or earth without the foreknowledge of God. An important part of the strategy which God has for today is that He wants to show that His power is not just in heaven, but also demonstrated very powerfully on earth.

We know that in His personal relationship with you, He loves, He heals, He forgives – you, personally. But there is something God wants more than your healing, more even than your salvation – what God wants right now is to see Jesus so powerfully exalted, so powerfully glorified, so that when He returns at His Second Coming – every knee shall bow and the whole world will worship at the name of Jesus – which is going to happen in the near future. Therefore this is a major spiritual issue now!

God wants to use you to bring glory to the name of Jesus! This means that there must come a time when we stop asking God for what He can do for us, and begin to ask what we can do for Him!

Our Christian lives need to change from the passive to the active. God wants to put power into *your* life. In the West many want to receive healing, finances – something for themselves. The Bible is full of promises that He will heal us – but *why*? Why did God heal my throat cancer? So that I would give my life for Russia and the glory of Christ! Why did God miraculously release me from a communist prison thirty years ago? So that I would travel the world giving the glory to Him – and win over 250,000 lost and dying souls into the Kingdom in only two years! Why must we give to God sacrificially? Not in order that we can receive thirty – sixty – a hundred times back – but because we love Him and want to glorify Him through giving to win lost and dying souls! The fact that He *does* give back is not the *reason* for the gift, but the *result* of our sacrifice! It is so important to get the *motive* right!

In Russia I teach the people more than how to receive healing, I'm teaching them how **they** can preach the Gospel and heal the sick. The most important result of my ministry is not the hundreds of thousands who repent, but the hundreds who become evangelists and pastors through my ministry.

I do not agree with those who tell me that God does not need me to preach the Gospel, that He can use anyone. The Bible is the evidence that God can only use the few – *'many are called, but few are chosen'* (Matthew 22:14). God had to reduce Gideon's army to only three hundred. Why? Because God can only use willing, obedient, committed people who will make His glory the first priority. God needs the right men and women in order to do what He wants, to bring glory to His Name, to bring deliverance to nations, to build His Church – He's looking everywhere, to find those through whom He can direct all His power, and energy into saving sinners.

If only you can fully understand the love that God has for the sinner. Why? First, He wants to save them from the fire of hell; second, because He needs them to fulfil His purpose in bringing the glory of Christ to the world.

Look how much of God's time and energy is directed towards saving the sinner! The lost sheep takes priority over the safe ones in God's plan every time! In my crusades I do not see the people as others might – all the energy and power of God is being concentrated at that moment on reaching these people's hearts, not merely their heads – I see individuals whom God desperately wants in the Kingdom because I know what God wants to do in their lives.

All of us once were sinners whom God loved, chose, fashioned and created. As an evangelist I know that when God looks at sinners, He doesn't just see alcoholics, drug addicts, the hopeless broken lives. What He sees is the potential, what you can be when He touches you! God is always seeing the future. When you were still a sinner, God saw something in you He wanted. Sometimes it takes a long time – with Moses it took eighty years to form the real man that God could use to do the job! If only you knew what God sees in you, if you could see yourself as He sees you, not as you see yourself! What a difference it could make in your life if you would recognise your potential with God!

When God deals with you, He does something unique. So often we want what other people have. In my relationship with God, I have never wanted what somebody else has. I want what is in His Word, what God has for me personally! Don't copy other people. If you want the power of God, that power is not going to come from somebody else. Yes, others can lay their hands on you, but the power is going to come from God. Not from me, nor from someone else. You must get it direct from God and His Word.

I was only fourteen when I was baptised in the Holy Spirit. What I wanted was what was in the Bible, the baptism of fire, of power. I knew that when the fire came down on a hundred and twenty people in the Upper Room, they became fiery evangelists – and immediately Peter held the first evangelistic crusade of the early Church!

You see, they were searching for God, waiting expectantly! And on the day of Pentecost, the miracle happened – the same Holy Spirit that had transformed Jesus, the same dynamic power that turned Him from the carpenter's son into the Son of God, the same power that raised Him from the dead – this same power came on the first church, changed their lives and suddenly there was an explosion of evangelism, thousands of people saved – people who had come to Jerusalem from all over the world to celebrate the Jewish festival of Pentecost – these were the ones who found the reality of salvation, the miracles of healing – and now these were the ones who went out in the power of the Holy

Spirit to spread the news of salvation worldwide. First evangelists, then missionaries! The same explosion can happen today!

When I was searching for the baptism of the Holy Spirit, I wanted something explosive that would change my life. If you do not want that – if you want a quiet life, enough money to buy your food, some nice clothes – you will get what you want, but nothing more!

I'm always needing and expecting more of God's power. Yes, I have a vision for Russia and Ukraine. Twelve years ago I was the first evangelist to take the Dynamo Stadium in Kiev for evangelism, and I prophesied from Jeremiah 33:6–9 that God would bless and change the whole nation. I believe that what has happened *now* is the fulfilment of *that* prophetic vision.

This is only the beginning – what has happened in Ukraine can happen in Europe. I want to see more of the power of God on earth than any man has ever seen! Why? Because I don't want to limit God! I have a vision of a God who is so much bigger than you or I can ever imagine! The God of the Bible has so much more power, is so much bigger, more glorious, more exciting than anything you could dream about! So start dreaming, but then stop dreaming and start to do something!

God **needs** men and women who want to see His power, His glory, who want to see God in **action**! God needs **you** because He can only fulfil His plan through you or me.

And if God does not do it through you, He will do it through somebody else. When I was a young man, I had to get a job in a London City bank to raise the money to go to Bible College. I was very impatient; I wanted to be an evangelist. I was so worried, I used to pray, 'I know what You want me to do, but while I am working in this bank, please God, don't give my job to someone else!' Have you ever prayed like that?

Jesus said, '*You did not chose Me, but I chose you*' (John 15:16). If you are a leader, a man or woman of God, it was not your choice. God chooses the people He knows and can trust, who will not quit when it gets tough, and who will not accept the way things are, but believe for the miraculous.

If you know without any question that the call of God is on you, then God will do something dramatic in your life. Get yourself ready spiritually for that moment! I am determined that I am going to get what I want from God! Stop dreaming, get into *action*, now!

Do you want to be where God is? Do you want the power of God? Then go where God is telling you, do what God is telling you. If you don't, the fire of God will move on and you will be left with nothing. Go with the fire. Do you want spiritual revival? – If you don't evangelise, revival will not come! People of God, get out and evangelise, God is telling you, Go now! If you don't, your church will stop growing and the power of God will leave.

Ask God for miracles and He will do them. But it's **you** who must evangelise – you don't need me or another evangelist – **you** do it right where you are!

Be warned, if you do not take your nation for Christ, the devil will – and the devil's plan is worse than anything you can imagine.

We Need the Spirit Elijah Had!

Elijah could be called the greatest evangelist in the Bible (excluding Jesus), because he is the only man who could bring a whole nation to repent in one day. Elijah is an example to me, and I want to find the secret of his power, to learn how he could do what he did.

In the time of Elijah Israel was in rebellion against the only real God – as Russia also was under communism. The European Union today is in a similar rebellion against God. The Council of Europe produced a poster – based on the painting of the Tower of Babel – to promote the EU. Then they opened a new Parliament building in Strasburg (December 2000), based on the same painting. I asked them in Strasburg, 'Do you know this Parliament is a replica of the Tower of Babel?' And they said, 'Yes, we want to finish what we failed to do 3,500 years ago!' According to the Bible, the Tower of Babel was built as the symbol of man's rebellion against God – but why is the same symbol at the centre of the European Union? Christians should be on their knees crying out to the God of the Bible – lest they become identified with the gods of Babylon!

In the Bible the history of Israel shows how many times they forgot their God and began to adopt and worship other gods. God had to constantly bring them back to repentance. But where is the power of God in our land? Why do we cry out for a spiritual revival? Are we in danger of putting other gods before the Lord our God? Does the Church need repentance again today?

I want to know the God of Elijah! He had such authority, he called the whole nation together and then he gathered the false prophets of Baal. Elijah was not afraid to call all those who opposed him, all the demon possessed, to come. Then he said, 'Let's demonstrate whose God is real – your gods or my God!' (see 1 Kings 18:21). And the power of God came down with fire, because Elijah knew not only how to pray with authority, but how to get an answer to prayer. Suddenly I find here is a man so different, who knew the mind and will of God, and could act so dangerously that if he failed, King Ahab, if not the prophets of Baal, would kill him, or worse still, Jezebel would!

Elijah challenged the prophets of Baal – because he really believed that literal fire would fall from heaven and burn wood, water and the flesh of the sacrifice! Not just a spiritual experience, not falling on the floor or a vision, but literal fire – heavenly fire that is going to literally burn wood, water and sacrifice. He believed that God would do that. But nobody had ever before spoken to God with such faith and authority in such a dangerous situation!

Now, if we are living in the days of Elijah, and if you want the spirit of Elijah – prove it! Do something that nobody else can do, something nobody else has ever done before. Demonstrate a power and authority with God like he did!

Elijah started with dry wood, then commanded them to dig a trench all round, pour twelve big barrels of water over the whole sacrifice, so even if it was possible to have fire before, it's not possible now! Elijah made it impossible for God to answer his own prayer! But look at the words, how Elijah prayed:

> 'Hear me, O LORD, hear me, that this people may know that You are the LORD God . . .'
>
> (1 Kings 18:37)

That's the challenge! It's time we got to know the real God, the God of the Bible, the God of power, the God of miracles. Elijah is saying, 'Lord, hear me, so that the people will know two things.

Firstly, that you are the true God, and secondly that they will know that you have forgiven them.' Elijah is not actually praying for fire. He says, 'Oh God, demonstrate to the unbelievers so powerfully that the whole nation will repent.'

I understand that mission societies regard a nation as unevangelised if there is only one per cent or less of real believers. In the whole enlarged European Union there are fewer than one per cent real born-again believers – so we should be classed as unevangelised! That is the situation we are in! Do you see why it is so important to look at this seriously?

With Elijah, immediately after he prayed, the fire came down and burnt up the wood, the sacrifice and the water – everything! Now that is God. It was a miracle.

But this was only the beginning. The reason that King Ahab wanted to kill Elijah was because Elijah had prayed for the rain to stop and there had been no rain in Israel for three and a half years. Now God has sent the fire, the whole nation has repented, and Elijah prophesies that God is going to send rain.

I find some very unusual things about prayer in the Bible. I don't read that Elijah went away for forty days and prayed – but he is about to see another, bigger miracle than the fire! He says to Ahab, *Go up, eat and drink; for there is the sound of abundance of rain!'* (1 Kings 18:41). But Elijah can't hear it. Ahab gets up to eat, and Elijah goes off to the top of Mount Carmel (1 Kings 18:42). No, the Bible doesn't say he is fasting and praying. It says he got down on the earth, he put his head between his knees, then got up and commanded his servant, 'Go up and look towards the sea. Look for the rain.' The servant says, 'There isn't any.' Seven times he sends his servant to look for the rain (see 1 Kings 18:43). You see, Elijah is living dangerously. When he said to King Ahab, *'Go up, eat and drink; for there is the sound of abundance of rain,'* Elijah had not seen the rain. There was no evidence – but he knew God, and to me it is almost as if something strange is happening. It's not because Elijah is praying, but he knows in his heart, he knows that God will send the rain.

All Elijah had to do was to say, 'Oh God, I need another miracle, do it again!' And God answered him. The more I read this in the Bible, the more I feel that I myself haven't got the answer yet. Three and a half years before Elijah simply said, 'Ahab, no rain' and the rain stopped. Then he calls upon God, 'Show Your power.' Fire comes down. Now he says, 'There's going to be another miracle, there's going to be rain' – but there is no evidence at all! I don't find a record of long prayers, but of a man who knows God. I have noticed something quite unusual: sometimes the shorter my prayer, the quicker the miracle. When you know it is going to happen, you speak the word and God does it.

We need to be more like Elijah. We have a prayer-answering God, but do we really believe Him? Do we believe the power of God? Well, if we do, then we must act. Faith is where your feet go, faith is what you do. But you can only be like that if you know God.

Do you know what the spirit of Elijah is? To me it is the power that a man can have with God. If you knew the power that you can have, you can call down fire from heaven, see a nation repent in a day, command the rain to come and it will – that's the power that God has given you. I will prove it from Mark's Gospel:

> 'Now in the morning, as they passed by, they saw the fig tree [that Jesus had cursed] dried up from the roots. And Peter, remembering, and said to Him, "Rabbi, look! The fig tree which You cursed has withered away." So Jesus answered and said to them, "Have faith in God. For assuredly, I say to you, whoever says to this mountain, 'Be removed and be cast into the sea,' and does not doubt in his heart, but believes that those things he says will be done, he will have whatever he says." '
>
> (Mark 11:20–23)

Jesus had just come from Bethany and was on the Mount of Olives, talking about the Mount of Olives being cast down into the Dead Sea! You read your Bible! Now, that's impossible. Jesus said, it isn't impossible, nothing is impossible. The strange thing is that we, as believers, and I have to include myself, do limit God. I want to tell myself, 'David, read these words. With God nothing is impossible. Nothing!' Then Jesus went on in verse 24: *'Therefore, I say to you, whatever things you ask . . . '* Listen – whatever you ask! Whatever you ask, whatever you pray – believe that you receive it and you will have it!

That is the spirit of Elijah – that's his secret! The Elijah who could stand on Mount Carmel, put water on the sacrifice – and leave it to God! I can just imagine Elijah doing it – there's the sacrifice and the water and Elijah stands back, waiting, and the fire comes. Just like that! Then he goes off to the top of Carmel and puts his head between his knees. The Bible doesn't even say he prayed. But God knew. God sent the rain. God sent the fire and the rain, because Elijah had a relationship with God – a relationship that you can have.

Do you want to see revival in Europe? All God needs is one man or woman who can pray like Elijah, who can believe like Jesus said. You will get big troubles – and big miracles. Don't be afraid. That's the price we have to pay.

Nothing is impossible with God. You only need the spirit of Elijah.

Eurovision Mission to Europe

Eurovision Mission to Europe was founded by David Hathaway when God literally gave him a vision for Europe.

As an evangelist, David's goal is to demonstrate who the *real* Jesus is. Everyone knows about religion, but many don't know *who* Jesus *really is* in the world today.

David's vision continues to grow and develop ... but God's purposes can only be fulfilled through the continued support of individuals and churches. David says, 'I will not stop until we reach the whole of Russia and Europe with the Gospel of Jesus Christ. It takes revolutionary, triumphant faith that will overcome every challenge. But with God – and your support – we can do it!'

David Hathaway invites correspondence which should be addressed to:

> Eurovision Mission to Europe
> 41 Healds Road
> Dewsbury WF13 4HU
> UK
>
> *Email*: office@eurovision.org.uk

Eurovision Mission to Europe is a Registered Charity, No. 1013288

In the USA please contact:

> Prophetic Vision USA Inc.
> PO Box 10565
> Wilmington DE19850
> USA
>
> *Email*: usa@propheticvision.org.uk
>
> Federal ID #452–2050718

For further information on David's ministry, books and videos please visit: www.propheticvision.org.uk

Prophetic Vision magazine

David Hathaway is editorial director of *Prophetic Vision* magazine which is published free of charge in English, German, Danish/Norwegian and is distributed to over 130 countries. Some editions are published in Russian, Ukrainian and Bulgarian. *Prophetic Vision* magazine has a readership of over half a million – one of the largest Christian readerships in the world.

The aim of the publication is to convey a strong prophetic vision for these end times. The Bible is so clear that in prophecy one can see the devil's strategy, but also God's strategy, what He wants to do to defeat the devil, save the lost and prepare for Christ's kingdom. This puts an awesome responsibility on us to evangelise the world *now*!

To receive your free copy please visit:

www.propheticvision.org.uk

Or contact:

Eurovision Mission to Europe
41 Healds Road
Dewsbury WF13 4HU
UK

Tel: +44 (0)1924 453693
Email: uk@propheticvision.org.uk

In the USA please contact:

Prophetic Vision USA Inc.
PO Box 10565
Wilmington DE19850

Email: usa@propheticvision.org.uk

David Hathaway's Books

The Power of Faith. David's personal testimony which he has shared all over Russia and Ukraine. This book will change your life, and then you too will experience the Power of Faith.

Why Siberia? Hundreds of miracles happened when God called David to go to the end of the earth – spiritual adventure – life on the edge – very humorous – compelling reading! A challenging call to missions today!

Czech-Mate. Best-selling account of David's Bible smuggling behind the Iron Curtain. Vivid portrayal of torture and triumph in a communist prison – midnight vision – answered prayer – dramatic release by Harold Wilson – faith in action!

Available on DVD and Video

The Rape of Europe. Many people think that the Bible is just history, or that it is full of prophecy about the future: this compelling documentary about the European Union will clearly show you that we are living in the time when prophecy is being fulfilled today – literally in your lifetime!

A full product list is available at:

www.propheticvision.org.uk